on Tuesday,

when the homeless disappeared

Camino del Sol
A Latina and Latino Literary Series

on Tuesday, when the homeless disappeared

poems by
Marcos McPeek Villatoro

The University of Arizona Press
Tucson

The University of Arizona Press
© 2004 Marcos McPeek Villatoro
All rights reserved

∞ This book is printed on acid-free, archival-quality paper.
Manufactured in the United States of America

09 08 07 06 05 04   6 5 4 3 2 1

Library of Congress Cataloging-in-Publication Data
Villatoro, Marcos McPeek.
On Tuesday, when the homeless disappeared :
poems / by Marcos McPeek Villatoro.
p. cm. — (Camino del sol)
ISBN 0-8165-2390-8 (pbk. : alk. paper)
1. Hispanic Americans—Poetry.
2. Appalachian Region—Poetry.
I. Title. II. Series.
PS3572.I386O5 2004
811'.54—dc22   2004003608

Publication of this book is made possible in part by the proceeds
of a permanent endowment created with the assistance of a
Challenge Grant from the National Endowment for the
Humanities, a federal agency.

Para mi vida—siempre Michelle

Contents

Que seas razonable, cabrón

One Tuesday, while driving home from my college, I passed a gentleman standing in the curve of Sunset and the 405 ramp. He had a sign. Rain had pulled the words down the cardboard. A grocery cart stood behind him. Some drivers gave him money. I had none. Perhaps tomorrow, I thought. Tomorrow I'd bring change.

Tomorrow came. His cart rested against the cement railing. But he was gone.

In the days following I happened upon other empty carts. One had its cardboard sign half-folded and crumpled into a corner. On Sepulveda I counted seven carts in a haphazard row. I stopped jogging and stared at them awhile.

"They're gone," I muttered. "They left us."

A ridiculous notion, of course. And the beginning of a poem.

I chose the sestina as the form. It's difficult, and I wanted to see if I could do it. Six stanzas make a sestina. You use the end words of each line over and again. Then in a final, shorter stanza (called an envoi) you fit all those end words into a smaller space. It's the *New York Times* crossword puzzle for poets. It raises the tennis net about three inches. Tough going, a sestina, and a lot of fun.

Having fun while writing a poem on the homeless. Do I want people to know this about me?

Ever since the day W. H. Auden said, "Poetry makes nothing happen," we poets have struggled. How can poetry be useless? Have not Václav Havel and Pablo Neruda roused freedom in Czechoslovakia and Chile? Maya Angelou's own witness to racism and poverty has made us, as a society, more aware.

Then again, those famed poets wrote about their people's struggle through beautiful verse. Pain may have birthed the poem, but it was art that made the pain ironic, poignant, beautiful.

My little poem will not give the gentleman on the 405 ramp a home. Nor will it start any movement to eradicate homelessness in L.A. Yet the human desire to write verse lingers.

Overall I agree with Mr. Auden. We don't write poetry to make something happen. A poem is not a memo; rhymed verse doesn't

1

mean to say "You've got mail." Very little will change with the composing of a line of iambic pentameter. We write a poem, not to send a message, but simply because we must write a poem: we must come to know ourselves.

Yet my only cavil with Mr. Auden is this: if anything, poetry helps us to pay attention. Very close attention. A man stands on the 405 ramp at Sunset, while I drive home.

False Memory

To turn to the source
    Is difficult. Not for reasons
Of pain nor denial
    But rather the fear
Of the tedious, an eye
    Toward the crowd.
Are they bored? Will they
    Turn another away, will
Their coins clatter
    In another man's jar?
Then comes the scold,
    The reminder, the reason
We do all this. A search
    For the purity, found in
The past. What a laugh.

Interpretation

For Susan Sontag

Too much metaphor
    For that young woman on the bus
Who wept when the Mexican boy sang.
    The boy is not a symbol. He is poor.
Poverty means nothing. I used the word
    This morning, driving my daughter
To an advanced art class. "We were too poor,"
    I said, "to buy our own books.
Your grandmamma would take me to the library."
    And she: "You were poor?" and though Emily knows
Nothing of the boy on the bus in Vera Cruz
    Who sang a norteño to my student
And made that woman weep, my daughter doubts me.
    For I have told her before about poverty,
Have tried to shape images for her: dead children
    In a Guatemalan village, the little bodies
That I touched—for touch was a simulation
    Of caring: let the grieving mother
Know I cared. It was a sleight of hand,
    A way for me to touch the thing I feared:
The child was me. A metaphor. The twenty-three-inch corpse
    That grayed with the temporal, that turned
Inert with smells that made the mother turn
    Away, became my simile. Love is like
Oxygen. Mornings are like a barrel of monkeys,
    And that mother is nothing like me.
Emily, nine years old, if allowed into this,
    Could point that out quickly: a grieving mother
In a humid village couldn't be like me, not without
    A library card. She wouldn't mean
To be ironic. She doesn't mean
    To ask for meaning. Emily wants to know
What poverty is, and I have failed to say.

She's used to that. She's accustomed to
A man who kisses her warm on the forehead
    And makes cereal boxes explode with a sudden fist,
All in one day. Doors slam through her,
    Voices tighten over her whenever he fails
As father. And yet she asks the questions,
    She wants to know about that bus
And the crying woman and the singing boy
    Who called you *maricón,* then held your hand
When you walked out and saw the castles
    Of his hometown. Poor, you said,
Then you gave him a name—Jose Luís, age nine,
    Emily's age. It's not a lie. He's nine.
Boarding a bus with strangers. Making gringas weep
    For a price. Collecting dollars
From each one of us. Smart. Savvy. Poor.
    Libraries instead of bookstores. Three-foot-long
Coffins instead of cartoons. An art class
    On a Saturday morning. And here
You struggle, in these final lines: it's a wrap. No:
    It's an interpretation. That's why you fail.

On Tuesday, When the Homeless Disappeared

No doubt that we'd become a happy lot.
We had a lot of dough. When I drove home
I'd hand a wad to the guy with the sign
On Sunset and the ramp. There was his cart,
But he was gone. He had folded the words
Into a cardboard airplane. No other message

Of his whereabouts. But I need messages
And paper trails. Of that we have a lot.
We have free access to many words
And worlds. We take the freeway home
But of course we pay. That's why we don't have carts.
That's why we never need a cardboard sign.

It was a Tuesday when we saw the signs
Of disappearance. All those cardboard messages
Abandoned in rusted, badly parked carts
Strewn before libraries, in realtor parking lots.
One wry fellow said, "Perhaps they went home."
I smudged my fingers with the smear of words.

Then one among us got cellular word
Of someone who went public. Yet another sign!
There was no reason for us to go home,
Not with new emails bringing the message
Of a really great buy. We quit the lot.
The cardboard settled back into the cart.

A Bird-of-Paradise bloomed through a cart
Near the Getty. No cardboard. But its beauty hushed our words.
All the Wilshire artists cast their lots
To be the one to paint a cardboard sign.

The *L.A. Times* cast us a fine message:
"In art our homeless finally find a home."

We still weren't sure, as we drove home
Where all those people who once pushed carts
Had gone. Would they need their cardboard messages
In their new dwelling? Or perhaps such words
Were useless. Again, too many signs
Told us that we should celebrate our lot.

Yet in one cart of a Starbucks parking lot
Near a Brentwood home, they found a cardboard sign.
It had no message. Not one written word.

The Odor

Put your nose right there against the wall
And you will smell
Mango. Not one, but an orchard.
Yet this is stucco. That is a desk
And these are books. This is where
The writer has fallen and he offers no apologies.
He comes here every single day and sits.
He brings folded lunches. Yesterday
He brought the mango but forgot his knife,
The one he carried in El Salvador
Where he used it daily against
Corn stalks and flathead screws
And mangoes. These days
It slips through envelopes,
Then lays closed and forgotten
Aside the paper clips and old receipts.
Then there's today, when the stucco and the lamp
Pulse with the sap of shallow-rooted trees.
The mango sits aside the coffee pot
More reddish than yesterday, a blush
Of maturity. The air
Tumbles from the room into the hall.
He closes the door against the world,
Presses his face against the wall.
He piles the filing cabinet with socks,
A tie, the striped shirt, the white underwear.
He unfolds the blade,
Presses his shoulders against the wall, slices
Through the wet strings, slips the orange meat
Over his tongue, then slips himself
Into the loosened peels.

Mask

Today I will consider Tekún Umán
Whose wooden face hangs on my office wall
For all the passersby to ask "Who's that? Who is he?"

And I can tell the dead Indian's story,
Of how he was the last Mayan to fall
In the flu-ridden skirmishes with the Spanish,

And how he and I hold one thing in common—
My birthday is on his commemoration—
And thus the smile weaves over my humble face

For I have made clear all political positions
By standing behind the wooden mask of a dead man.
When the visitors leave, they do not notice

That I shut the door and dim all the lights
And take the wooden sculpture from the nail
And run my finger down the groove of his cheek,

The large bump over his nose, wondering
If the woodcutter thought that necessary
To render satisfied our concepts of a native;

Which as well goes for the multi-plumed quetzal
That sits on his crown. Its feathers
Swoop down and cover his ears. The bird has no

Color except brown. Its eyes reflect his own—
Large, open, empty—honest as a mask.
Of course I try it on. I press the curve

Of its backing against my confused face
And dance a fine rain dance, back and forth
Across my white carpet, newly shampooed.

Zazen Interruptus

One

Of course it stands alone
And thus there is desire
That digs a hole, a place to square my head
And hide. The earth smells good today.
Dead caterpillars make a hearty musk.
Those cat feces of yore
Threaten no passing pregnancies.
Don't follow those women. They are too obvious.
They walk from shoe stores to adulterous husbands
Who will weep on delivery, then make promises to God.
Stay with your hole, sir. I dare you.
Ignore Yorick's splinters. Ignore that T-bone.
Yes, the shovel cleft the slate. It left you
A corrugated timeline, yet another entertainment.
And then this trick: don't bother with the air.
It swamps the hole. I dare you.
Breathe, of course. You may count the breaths,
Each one, one.

Meditation

The concern
Is that Jesus may get lonely
Thumbing a ride on
Van Nuys and Sepulveda
Considered between
First and fifth gears
A brief meditation in a breath
When breathing as you know from all that reading
On Siddhartha and the Big Mind of zazen
Is fundamental is the one samsaric act
That can break the cycle that you now breathe
Between second and third dodging the used Mercedes
That pulls out of Vesper Avenue
A street where drug deals flow like emptied pool water
Which explains the Mercedes except you know that driver
She cleans the sanctuary on Thursdays she sends her daughter
To first communion classes with Raquel
And she leaves early every morning toward a mop
That leans in a closet corner in Hewlett-Packard
And the Mercedes is used and it's October
And there are deals in dealerships all through the Valley
For poor folks like her
Poor folks there's a lesson
Perhaps in a second breath
The solitude may dissipate
And you can stick to your rules
About hitchhikers

To Enku

Enku asked a friend to bury him
upright with a reed in his mouth
through which he breathed chants until
the prayers ended and an oak grew there
entwined with wisteria vines
that the locals dare not cut

This only after sixty years of carving
Buddhas into cedar logs
and Shintos out of cypress
which was not enough not enough at all
he collected the splinters
and carved piles of chip-Buddhas
for children who watched the same axe
that drew the dreary face of a deity
from a log now slice the god
free from a splinter

It all ended the day
he finished three sets of gods for villagers
in the Hida province
chopped the words of an old promise
One hundred thousand Buddhas completed
then dropped the axe beside the river grave

and breathed his life out through a bamboo reed
none of which I understand as meditation
what with the sweat of carving and the song of dying
while sitting in your own grave
ringing a bell against that pile of earth
that chokes off all those years of action

as if death had already come along
with the carved words

a self-abnegation
that is pure and clean as the sweat
on the axe handle

as though action and meditation
were of the same cut
that both had begun
with the first block of wood
where he coaxed Siddhartha from the grain
and this is why the locals fear the vines
that bleed whenever pruned
as if they know the meditation
never ended

The Familiar

I

Forgetting is an act of human will.
An animal does not forget the smell
Of a blood trail, nor the track of thunder
Through the trees. It's the smell of survival,
The sound of another day existing,
Something I have forgotten. There was a time
When the words ripped through this open page
With the human shriek that I had called
Familiar, what I had termed necessary.
The darkness of centuries, the black hope
Of another language, another darker blood.

II

As we ran into evening, my lungs pumped
The fear away. It was a true dark,
A black that had no edges, except for trees
Whose limbs bent round the edges of my eyes.
We were few, and most of us were young,
Brown in the bone. Shadows ourselves.
We had done something wrong. We had committed
Acts of egregious, traitorous impiety,
Which made us slap each others' backs and smile.
The lights ruined our shadows. They had lanterns
And large pickup trucks. Their dogs knew us
By our accents. The men's faces, pink and stained
With camouflage, shined with the sweat of the hunt.
They were real dancers. Look how they swung
Their lamps like clubs. Hell of a night, boys.
Darkies in the dark. You can't beat that.

The Deer

Nicaragua, July 1985

From tiny villages
Of morning tortillas,
Where a man bathes in the river
Before leaving home
For the day, where a woman
Stands at his door, her shiver

Scarcely hiding worry;
Where pigs ignore fences
And a soldier ignores his fear
Of the mountains
He left last night, shuffling
Toward a mother angered to tears;

Upon the stony road
That runs through wet jungles,
Past smoky thatched shacks
And simple, one-room churches
Where an elder man packs
Clay into bullet holes;

Through early morning dew
The truckbed bounces south
Kicking us off our feet.
A baby almost flew
Out of her mother's hold.

A boy laughs. He rolls his eyes
At this world. He stands
To my left. He has much to prove,
Passing death in such stride,
Leaving her in church walls.
He stands right next to me.

I ride in the middle.
The thin fog penetrates
The woman's shawls. The babe
Sucks at warm milk. The rest
Rub the bumps into our arms
And contemplate the harm:

Our eyes follow the fog
Through pine and malinche,
Beyond a silent bog
So recently disturbed
By boots. The snapped reeds
Bend in forced genuflection

Toward the mud. They were tired;
The sole explanation
To leaving blatant clues
Out of broken stems.
We take consolation
In their absence.

A woman contemplates
While gazing at the mire,
"Or maybe they rushed away."
The truck grinds to slow our day,
To miss a rock, or perhaps
To rouse her desire

Concerning the living.
The arrogant boy
Stops laughing. A young man
Clutches a girl's fingers.
They glance toward the forest.
The truck turns left, then right,

Cutting a crescent moon
Into the billowed road.

A man lets go his hold
Of the truckbed's railing.
He opens a small sack
And hands us oranges.

We smile at his kindness.
Though it means to appease,
We take the fruit and listen
As he fakes the ease
Of accepting Eternity:
He mentions many names.

Some of those names I know.
We carried them all
To the town plaza,
Placing the larger pieces
In a bloody row
That families passed, collecting.

"Pues sí . . ." that peculiar
Affirmative, ". . . pues sí."
Passengers let go their breaths.
One woman crosses herself
To bless those recent deaths
Or perhaps to bless the truck.

The trucker's sudden brake
Jolts us toward the cab.
He steps onto the road
And stares into the fog.
We also see the beast
Stepping over a log.

The deer stands at attention.
Its rack towers into two
Wooden laurels. Their tips
Almost touch. Its neck

Holds the crown still. Its eyes
Hold our crowd still.

"Qué bello," someone whispers.
We nod our heads, a herd
Of mammals in a cattle truck.
Even I forget the reeds,
Broken, until a word
Snaps over the trucker's lips.

He rushes a step forward,
Lifts a hand to the deer.
"No." Then he stops, knowing
his movement will cause movement,
his warning will create flight.
Where he turned left, then right

Is where one hoof now stands,
Right in the crescent moon
Of the billowed road.
The trucker whispers
Curses like a prayer
And turns away.

We do not understand.
We learn quick enough
As he turns the motor
And a sharp, kicked puff
Follows a wire's click
That our driver avoided

With a crescent moon.
The deer cannot be seen,
Except for shattered laurels
That snap through thicker fog.
Then there's the acrid smell of deer
In the fog's gun-powdered sheen.

El Salvador, 1932—1981

I

Witness

Before the trumpet sounded, before
Anyone needed to lift their skulls, before
There was a reason to mention any of this,
God touched the head of a fly named Martínez.
A bug that wore laurels. It confused the folk.
So they called him El Brujo, for only a witch with balls
Could get away with all this.

He announced La Limpieza.
"Papá knew nothing of The Cleansing. He
Rushed into the room
To scoot us out the door.
We hid in a cornfield
Where mamá kept a finger
In my baby brother's mouth.
Then the rattling, it began.
I first thought those were cornhusk dolls
Kicking over the tassles, leaping
At a full moon.
My family huddled between two rows.
I crawled to the edge to watch
The dolls become bodies and drop into a ditch.
Women leapt over the bank
To join their husbands.
Children jumped to follow their mothers.
Soldiers sat on the bulldozers.

"I crawled away to other stalks
Across from the plaza.
Two soldiers played soccer with skulls.
Five soldiers worked to make more balls.

They grabbed clumps of hair, drew machetes, and chopped.
They grabbed clumps of hair, pulled back,
Chopped, flung heads, snatched hair,
Chopped tossed snatched,
Chopped, tossed, and
Snatched again."

Should this be told any other way?

"'This is too fucking slow!'
The rattle beat against my cheeks.
I heard one end, another begin,
Like thick chains falling on the plaza.

"I saw the children.
They trembled five feet away from my stalks.
If I could reach through the corn
And touch their shoulders, if I could grab
The waists of their pants.

"'I can't kill kids,' a voice said.
The commander slapped the soldier,
Snatched a baby by the neck,
Tossed her up like a heavy coin
And held the rifle erect.

"Papá's whisper wished to scream
At me. His hand
Flapped between corn at me, at me.
But I mowed down the stalks,
Snapping down a row an acre long.
Water woke me.
I slept.

"To my left moved
The hump of a woman's back.
Her shoulders pushed against the ground.

26

I could not see her head.
She had survived decapitation.
I yelped when
The shoulders lifted from the earth,
Hauling a face from a hole in the ground.

"She whispered, 'Don't scream girl.
Don't cry. Don't scream.'

"A warm arm wrapped my shoulders.
She pushed my head into the hole.
I could not see the morning light.
I smelled the humid earth.
I heard her gentle commands
Repeated above me, *'Now child,*
Go ahead. Cry. Scream, child.
Right in there.'"

II

The Phoenix of the Guanacos

I saw her in the distance, in her time
As she snatched at wind, gathering whispers
In a canasta of dried beans and corn.
She barely smiled my way, so busy,
Knocking sunshine into the frying pan.
She spoke her language, and though I did not know
The meaning, I recognized the cooking.
The tortillas raised up in hot protest
Like nervous clams. The blood, up to her knees
Couldn't trip her dance. As the brown vision
Whipped away I wondered if she listened
To a rhythm of hope or madness
Echoing in the hollow wind that passed
Over the lips of nineteen thirty-two.

Guanaco: The nickname for the people of El Salvador.

The Scold

Five candles flickered in the cornfield
The curandera was at her work. She had lit them.
A lowrider with Guadalupe decals and tinted windshields
Left her here. With a casual turn of her neck
She called to me. I did not move. Her heart was large.
The wrap of her huipil, her callused thumbs, were rare here.
She did not speak. The candles said it all.
The pink worm of ambition cut a path down my spine.
I moaned and wept then laughed.
She blew them out, except the middle one.
"This one is god." She ignited incense
In a paint can. "The end of your world does not stop his."
She tied the can with chords and whipped the air with smoke.
This was not like her, to scold. Then she left me
And my world is blank. It is cold and the air is still.

The Holy Spirit of My Uncle's Cojones

No one ate peyote like Uncle Jack.
He chewed the desiccated cactus meat,
A young raptor that slowed his grind only
While smiling at the dull special effects
Of my world, which failed to ruin his.

He broke all the sacred laws, drinking Beam
From the bottle and smoking homemade joints
Thicker than his electrician's thumb.
They were rolled from the best grass given him
By a Mexican *chota* who had procured
The bags from postmortem drug dealers.
Jack chewed forest mushrooms like a rabbit,
Then howled at a California night
While whispering *querida* above open thighs.
He dodged bullets from jealous husbands
(Save the one lodged beneath his scapula)
And radiator grills of six ex-wives.

Mamá dropped me off
Under a disco ball, when Castro Street offered
Bloodless liberation, and bell-bottoms
Dusted the streets. Jack stood, a brown stone of Salvador
On a San Francisco avenue.
In his Mustang I was added refuse,
Along with doobies that littered the rug
Like expired fireflies, and prescription bottles
Honoring various cultures:
Osegueda, two at every meal.
Johnson, avoid alcohol.
Smith-Perez, don't use heavy equipment.
They rolled like tiny maracas.
Jack kicked into gear over Market Street
And flipped me into his *café con leche* world.
Ey sobrino man, huele la concha.

He grinned as the wire-framed sunglasses
Decorated the blood that shot his eyes.

Different from the blood that pooled in my sink
Back in a distant Appalachian lair
Moist with incestuous kin.
                              "Forget this disco shit."
He had the Mustang sing me Los Lobos.
We flicked roaches through the window's crack,
Marking the trail toward Nevada.

In Reno he slipped a crisp bill between my fingers
And pushed me through legal doors.

The money was sufficient
To have her smile. *Suéltate* I heard
Jack's voice, *suelta*. Let the ropes come
Undone. Then he was gone.
Then she got down to work,
Making young boys forget
Stropped blades, far away.
                              Nothing strange
About this sex: consenting business partners,
Transient, agreed upon, done. Nothing strange,
Even when she touched that wrist
And asked about the *tajo*.

Through the thin walls I heard another:
The woman breathing like I breathed
As Jack's holy spirit swelled in her.

Afterwards he leaned against his hood,
Sunglasses on, arms wrapped over
A thick chest. His grill of teeth filtered a laugh,
Recognizing on my oily face the residue
Of consumed fruit, empty melon husks,
Stripped cobs, a spoon licked clean,

32

Then licked again.

Sabroso, ¿verdad?

The Mustang kicked us far and away.

• • • • •

When word got to me twenty years later,
With the news that Jack had died of natural causes,
I checked the wound that never learned the term
Suelta. A permanent rope strapped upon the skin,
A white chord on an olive terrain.

I feel it on my wrist, as though
A tiny, thin soul has perched there.

In the mornings I write.
During the day I work. On warm afternoons
The children and I make faces, chase giants,
Toss piles of books from one room to another.
She and I, monogamous. Nothing new
About this sex. It is not her fault.
At night
I drink zinfandel and turn the pages
Of a safe thriller or an upright novel.
Two glasses are enough to snuff the dreams
Of pale relatives.
Natural causes.
I wear a seatbelt all day. Watch my caffeine.
I eat like a gringo: yogurt, oranges,
Paul Newman nonprofit salad, bottled water,
And not one mushroom in sight.
I pretend to pray before the children
Who lip-sync my faith.
I glance about, hoping
To find a consenting smile, along with a whisper
Suéltate. Suelta. Nothing strange. Come
Undone.

The Snow

You pull out frozen pupusas
And warm them on the comal
That mamá hauled across three borders,
Under two platoons of M-16s
And before one LAPD blue
Who rested his eyes in coffee steam.
She looked harmless enough.
She slipped it through five decades,
Slid it over your stove,
Dropped wet masa harina
Into your hands.

¿Quién te puso tan chele vos?
The pupusa crumbles through your fingers.
The queso de cabro falls upon the stone,
Just like snow upon a dormant field.
Chele, chele sizzles with the cheese.
Ojalá. How to snap the metaphor
Of dilution?

Mixed-blood, half-breed,
Café con leche. Pupusas and yogurt.
Don't be a prick, pendejo.
It's all the same trick
You keep falling for. You keep tiptoeing
From comal to comal, flat stones
Over a thousand acres, afraid to wake the snow.

Mother

The sheets wrap tight her legs.
His knee locks her pelvis.
His face presses against her ear.

The other falls back. He's exhausted
From a feed that began
Hours ago, when the sweating corn
Sprayed the sun and baked us all to sleep.

His lips have popped away, leaving
The full round to swell into that tip,
Where her thin peach cloth covers
Nothing. She pulled the cloth herself.

She wanted all this, these boys
Holding her down, their eyes closed
To a dawn that makes its way
Into her shadows, the four soft plates

Of her abdomen, their oblique turn
That slips into the wet sheet.
This I pass between the coffee
And the computer, in this, my hour,

Now interrupted. My cup cools
While I stand in the hall, waiting—
For what? They, they all, are locked.

Skull Against the World

Your forehead knows all types of wood:
The dark oak desk, the pine of window panes,
The cedar chest that's safely put away
From infant's fingers; you have stood

And hit them all. Or you have jerked
And caught the rosewood of the crucifix
With your left ear. The bookshelf has you vexed.
All corner tables you have worked

To avoid. Still, they find you.
A wheeled toy is the mode of sabotage,
A beloved stuffed animal, lodged
Between the kneeler and the pew.

You leap to catch them, as if lives
Depended on the toy. This may be true;
Life without Max the Hippo would not do.
Yet must you sling your skull in sacrifice

To save that ragged doll? No sound
Is as frightful as a skull against the world
Even for children's sake. Their joy unfurls
Through the cultivation of your wounds.

Their ignorance is pure, planted
In bloodless bruises, ragged strips of pain
Running through a mother's mind. Again,
Must one be taken for granted

To save childhood? One final blow
Against your head may be of memory:
While they live woundless lives, they never see.
They will not know. They will not know.

The Cough

The children make of it a toy.
The four of them stand in a square
And play tubercular hacky-sack.
The girls use it as an offbeat patty cake.
The boys wipe its remnants
Onto the model car, shining the fenders.
Simon says gag.
They do so in unison, then
Break into a song of
Viscid harmonies.
In hide and seek
They billow the bedsheets.
It makes for an easy game.

At night they settle into piles of pillows.

It plays.
It kickballs their dreams.
It shows them their world after dark,
Forcing their heads into the toilet.
It makes of them a toy,
Squeezable dolls that produce
The most fascinating
Oil slicks on
Water.

Gotcha

Sometimes there is nothing to follow.
These tricks of this trade won't find a father
In a daughter's pain. She is abandoned.
He left her with tangled hair, in a pool
At the Y. The other children laughed
And he laughed too—the recipe for shame.

There is no other word for it but shame.
There are no sets of words that can follow
Humiliation, nor erase the laugh
Of the many. So when the father
Crosses his arms at the edge of the pool
She turns away. He has abandoned

His age. So easy it is to abandon
Goodness, a concept as lonely as shame.
The children dry themselves; she, in the pool
Wants to go under, where no one will follow,
But leave her to die there, where no father
Will lace his reprimand with hollow laughter.

There no one contaminates a laugh
With the spore of wrath. There she abandons
Breath and light. She sees a quivering father
Through water thick and heavy. It's a shame
You can't do it, girl. You're too young to follow
A need born in older years, when a pool

Takes on meaning. You can die in a pool.
You can fool them all: go ahead and laugh,
Right now. Down here. Then watch as they follow
The spasm of your joke. They'll abandon
Their sudden mockery. They'll drown the shame
With regret. Watch them. Watch him, the father

Swallow water all the way down. *Father,*
You'll say, *you blew it. The girl in the pool*
Is gone. Gotcha. Then watch as the shame
Ricochets. Go girl! Getting the last laugh
Like that. Getting them to abandon
All hope. Damn right. And oh how they'll follow

That father down. Down. How they'll follow
His trail through the pool, where they abandoned
A once-shamed girl who now, forever, laughs.

In the Hotel Room

Two for José David

This morning, in my hotel room, God cries.
It is a silent weeping. His thin lip
Trembles, thickens. His eyes thicken
With light, while I pack the briefcase and spray my neck
And gather the convention papers
In a swaddle. He's afraid.
I see this while scanning the room
For socks. His left shoe shifts toward the right,
Which is untied. These have been busy days.
I mean to teach him of the importance of my smile,
How I shake hands, how concerned I must be
Over my crossed legs, and how my fingers
Rest upon the interviewer's chair.
These are matters meant only for me.
Yet what I know he wants is attention.
A tousle of his hair, a flip over this bed
That he can freely jump on. Not like at home
Where I scold him for ruining the springs,
Showing him the other side of him, the lightning
And the hot stones. Not now. Just three flips,
Then a fourth. He on the bed, I will fall
To one knee and look up and open
My arms as if beholding glory
And catch him.

The Message

The hand upon his head.
A twist. Meaning to kiss
or debone: take the brain

from the bone. He'd be dead.
He knows this, so waits
for the message to clear.

He tries to remember:
pissing in the bedsheet,
crayon on the carpet,

his scrawled name on the door.
He feels the fingertips.
Not good. The palm is more

reasonable, an endearing
tousle, a simple
passing by. The tips

are spikes. They mean to stay.
They mean to pierce him
and lift him in one piece

straight around the brim
of those clouds, where Daddy says
God lives.

The Landlady

She spoke through a perfect box
Of teeth. She showed us the rooms
Of darkwood floors. She stood in a corner
Then moved when our eyes passed her,
Showing us the corner, like every other
Corner. She showed us how to turn on
Water. She took our money. She
Smiled. "Here is my face," she said. She pointed
To her caulky cheeks.
"You will know me by this face."

Then came Pati from Mexico. Our language changed.
That corner we filled with a dance.
The stained stove roped the air
From a folded tortilla. Cheese bubbled
Over the pan. My daughter laughed
At the pratfall twang
Of a snapped guitar string.
We giggled ourselves to sleep
Then kissed our brown skins awake.

We were fools to think of hot tortillas
As nothing more than food and gossip.
We did not feel the pressure on the walls,
Cold and thick, snow melting
Against our sizzle, crunching into ice.
Until she came. She ground us
In a perfect box of teeth.
She showed us the lease
Of hardwood laws. She stood at the door
And pointed. She squeezed our money.
From her screams
you'd believe she had blood.

The Elders

I

Dear Teilhard once said
The horizon is necessary
For the survival of sight.
I never read Chardin.
He was an old priest who had his moments.
(Get him to tell you how the evolving universe
Swirls perpetually into Christ's navel).
Still, he holds membership in that Boys' Club
Where Monsignor Mengano cracks a joke about theosophy
While pouring Teily three fingers of malt.
They discuss the value of balsa-wood women
Then turn silent before a passing acolyte,
His face like a girl's, and eyes that search
For a quick blessing.
I want no truck with them.
Nor have I come here for a cure
Regarding any vision.

Here, the ocean grips the outer corners of your eyes.
Night fingers the horizon. It pitches and folds
The light. This soon will pass. But the sand loads
The bottom of your sight. There are shadows
Where shadows have not been since yesterday
At this hour. Before you finish that glass
The sun will depart. The city behind us
Will replace it. For you and for me.

Its departure always leaves the silent lightning,
The unheard crack of twilight, where only
The quickest old men, chewing
Button-mushrooms the color of old snow, may enter.
They stand at the outer corner of our eyes.
No, I'm not afraid to go.
I've been near them, actually, in the strangest of lands
Far from here. (Take I-80 east to the cornfields.

You can't miss it).
I found the Mississippi
And her old men, the ones who curse the locks and dams.
One old fellow invited me for salad.
It happened some time after twilight.
Night became a cave in which clocks no longer function.
Language followed like a slapstick funeral procession.
Yes, his chimney spoke. What of it?
Its open hearth hoped to fellate me.
Don't tell me I'm afraid.
I must confess, I never found the crack
Between the worlds,
The one Teily and his boys
Talked about every single Sunday.
I did walk on the edge of shadows.
I tap-danced upon a shallow Mississippi splash.
The thought of a bird flew me over
Dubuque, upon which I almost pissed
Until the fear that some white guy
Would grab the ropy stream and pull me down.
That would have hurt.
Everything but twilight I could touch.
Naturally I sought a path.
Paths lead nowhere, one elder said.
He snatched my hand just as I leapt
Toward the river, where I meant to give in
To the Great Adventure. He knew better than I.
Earth's the right place for love, another old fart said,
Speaking to me, one who can't tell a birch
From a rhododendron.
I slid toward the waterline, tilted my head and listened.
Hard as hell, with that religious din
Barking at me through Teilhard's dry lips
Something about following The Way.
It has no heart, his rotting tongue flapped
Against the clenched coffin,
That path west has no real heart. Yet I swear I felt a pulse.

II

I barely hear the curates cursing me
In the name of the fodder and of the rum
And of the moldy spigot.
How dare I be so sly.
It's not a righteous dare.
They're far off, a good mile back
Just behind that line of newly planted palms.
They don't hear me mocking their swishing stoles
Nor the homilies, nor the wafer
(Have I mocked the wafer?).

At dawn upon the edge of this new road
I whispered a set of words,
A twenty-year-old stratagem that changed little.
"Grant me a restful night, a peaceful death,
The day I may be with you, ever closer."
Quite a bit more follows, a litany
Constructed by liberal theologians,
A smattering of campesinos
And the crumbling skeleton of parochial schools.

The old man came up from behind.
He popped a hard sponge between my lips.
I thought Eucharist. He laughed and shook his head.
Still, I genuflected
To years of line-item budgets,
Days of rosaries, weekends of reflection
Upon the ownership of ovaries.
Moments watching before early morning mass
Father splash holy water on the altar girl.
She danced in his rain. She laughed.
He watched her blouse turn sticky.
  They both were happy.

  I chewed and chewed and chewed
  And crossed myself a hundred twenty times.

III

Though the Mississippi swelled against the horizon,
The sky remained intact. Only the ice cracked,
Showing once again that God's domain
Will not be threatened by a metaphor.

Vos sos el Dios de los pobres, el Dios humano y sencillo.
El Dios que suda en las calles, el Dios de rostro curtido.

I once crammed myself into the skin
Of a ninety-five pound Nicaraguan man
Who carried corn sacks half his body's weight
Through a war zone of pine and coconut. I had learned to see
Through the eyes of an old woman patting tortillas,
Who wiped her hands on an apron
And walked to church pews of raw pine.
She leaned and whispered. Her dry fingers
Coated the beads, rubbed the corn dough
Into the dull, black finish.

I outgrew their skin.
Walked among a gentry who walked
Through cold that turned our faces gray.
We fondled one another with questions
And leaned over tables stained with latte rings.
Yes, I chose this. Hardly a velleity.

The sanctity of pain, one elder whispered,
Is a heresy. Someone told him that,
Then he told me. Never be afraid
Was another teaching. I know terror.
       I have quaked before happiness.
       I don't know what to do with it,
       Not with those corn-crusted beads,
       How they click click click.

IV

It has been silent. No one speaks.
We stand on beaches and stare
At the same horizon of water.
You should find your own spot.

The ocean holds the corners of my eyes
And I rest. After sunset I sleep.
No one walks the beach.
Even the old men do not pass.

Something tempts me.
Write a phrase about the poor,
Chant them a song to even the score.

Get quiet. Quiet.

Somebody just might come by.

The Plan

Their quick departure gave us
little time to study their ships or ask
about advanced propulsion systems
their thoughts on intergalactic wormholes their
reason for coming

It came out in a casual reference
to Christ and his influence upon their home
(you have him here too, so only a matter of time)
his birth happened thirty-seven-hundred years ago
and after his resurrection their people turned
to the yoke of science and philosophy
and they dedicated their entire selves
to something we didn't catch
he said all this while sipping
coffee through his third finger
and his second mouth somewhere between
Christ and philosophy whispered *How sweet!*
I must remember cappuccino
they left after the blitz torte

of course the Muslims laughed
as did all of Islam
no bombs went off for awhile
the Jews kept rather quiet
the *New York Times* showed a rabbi
with his arm around a priest
at the ninth hole
an evangelist ran for congress
on the Build Up NASA and Bomb Them to Hell ticket
theologians pondered our significance but soon they were shot
then a Jihad leader spoke on CNN
of our human arrogance
he referred to the visitors

and their smell-the-cappuccino proclamation
a pissed bishop said *well at least there is a Christ*
but no mention of a Buddha or Allah
that did it
the wars began soon after and soon after the wars
a few of us watched from the shadow of a burned Toyota
as the ships touched down once again
they walked out and looked about
that one with his finger in a
gallon of cappuccino kept muttering
between sips *well now*
this was easy

Mnemotics

I remember the day he walked in
And all the children in McDonalds died.

A desert town in California. 1984.
In Iowa I wrote a few lines

That had a few details: semi-automatic,
Two emptied cartridges, a third one full except

For the one bullet he gave himself, and saved himself
From us, who wanted his hide and his soul

And his sisters all dead. How he took away
Our sudden craving. That day I folded the paper

And dropped it on a bench. Found coffee and self-pity
And started writing. I would keep that man alive

In verse. I would write things to the world
That the world did not know. A shred of eighteen years

And this has changed. I click the mouse
And open menus. America's on-line. I'm on a line.

Such an exquisite corpse we are. So close are we
To one another. Every day I write to friends.

Small notes. Sometimes we chat in rooms
Filled with the most exciting people with the strangest names.

Now Iowa and desert towns meet on the same screen,
And I am fooled by information, a palimpsest

Of wisdom, a refraction of knowledge. I watch
The best minds of my generation hunched over

Pizza boxes and zip drives and other nostalgia
Of last month's catalog. The screen is flatter,

The images more mellifluous, the web sites, so animated,
They simulate our love for one another. They are true.

No time for regrets. No need to worry
For children who'd be now, what, twenty-eight?

Entablar

A veces sirven las palabras.
Me conmueve la justicia,
Nos toca la lucha.
Y yo no sé nada después de pasar
Días en una oficina, noches en un sofá
Llenos de vino y de libros.
Son mi alegría, pues.

Ya pasó una década.
No he oído nada de Chico.
Puede ser que Menchez, ya muerta.
Es el grito, fíjate, el aullido
Que pasa como la voz en una cueva,
Una grieta bien honda. Un hueco mío.

Es el joven que te promete la rabia,
Y lo dejamos, lo permitimos.
El joven no tiene ritmo, el joven
Coje el mundo como algo personal.
La lucha es íntima. La justicia significa
Un beso, dos tragos, tortillas para todos.
Después de años le decimos
Que se calme, que coja seguridad.
Firme aquí, señor. Tome esta, con comida.

Hace mucho tiempo que alguien
Ha ganado algo.
Es el éxito de una noche satisfecha,
La justicia del eructe.
No te rías.
Ya no conozco el lodo de la comarca.
Me da pena decir "vos."

Eso es para cuates. La seguridad
Es mi nuevo ataúd,
Y quepo bien. Pongo los brazos
Al pecho. Cierro los ojos.

La hija

Para Emily

Lee, la niña lee
Con sus piernas cruzadas,
Mujer naciente, linda y sexual
Por no saber, por no reconocer.
Es el libro en la mano
Que me hace delincuente,
Es lo malo de mi alma
Que me deja ver la inocente
Brotando con el olor
De la mujer ajena y distante.

Su pierna

Para Michelle

Ya han pasado tantos años,
       Las dos décadas que son nuestras,
Ladrillos de meses, la argamasa de los días.

Esa vena se ha hinchado. Pasa
       Por el lado de la pantorrilla;
Adentro, la sangre corre libre y caliente

Después de un partido de tenis, después
       De otro éxito. Palpita
Con el chorro de la batalla.

Más arriba, cerca de la orilla
       De los cortos azules, la piel es suave,
La telaraña roja, suave. No la siento.

Siento algo. Las yemas de mis dedos
       Se arrastran, queriendo hacerse
El susurro de un viento, una voz

En la cueva de su oído, una promesa
       subversiva, un compromiso que se desliza
Por los vericuetos de una mujer práctica, una mamá

Que cuida a los ojos de los cipotes, que no oigan
       Tales palabras, promesas eróticas.
Es un truco, pues. Nos hacemos jóvenes

De mentiras. ¿Cuál es lo misterioso
       De conocerse? Quitar lo hermético,
Matar el amor? No creo. O sí, creo,

Puesto que no sé. El toque recóndito

Es lo que busco. Y no lo encuentro
Conmigo, con estos huesos de cuarenta años,

Huesos de desconfianza, tuétano del mañoso.
　　　Los ligamentos de un hombre—Ay no.
No vas a encontrar nada aquí.

Allá, en la curva de un muslo,
　　　En el silencio de esa mujer
Tan modesta, tal vez, con tiempo

Encuentras la verdad de esta ilusión.

Vera Cruz, México

Para Raquel

Aquí la tierra se respira
De humedad. La noche nos lame
Y los indios nos miran sin la ira

Que merecemos. Ella no me llama.
Ella dobla la ropa que había bordada
En Chiapas. Nadie se inflama

De rencor. Nada nos recuerda
De los antepasados suyos, míos.
Solo hay ropa, negocio. La falda

Lleva un dibujo del río
Donde nació. Ella se ríe
Cuando digo *tzutzunil*, un lío

De sintaxis suelto. Sus pies
Son duros, y las sandalias
Pegan la acera, me pegan a mis días

Ya pasados, cuando un joven de varias
Creencias pegaba al mundo
Con gritos y con las plegarias

De justicia y de paz. Días profundos
Que clavaban el hombre con terror.
Días de balas y de huipiles, de pozos

Secos y un cipote sonriente. El error
Es la memoria. Aquellos cuentos
Ya no sirven. Es el esplendor

De su cara, los vericuetos rectos

De la mejilla, y su nombre
Que nunca sabré. Sólo un momento,

Y solamente otra India
        Que me sacude otra vez.
De cerca ella es tan fina,

Y yo soy otro gringo, pasando otra vez
        Comprando esta bolsa para mi hija.
Ella en su delicadeza

Me conoce. Me ve mejor que yo.
        El gringo que toca las obras
Y se atreve a bajar al precio

Ya bajo. Me conoce. Yo, no.

Fabiola

Ella llora por el niño machote
      Él que subió al bus de gringas
De sangre chicana. Ellas, que saben

Sin conocer, que han salido
      De muchos barrios, tantos hogares,
Que hablan el español de Los Angeles—

Para ellas, el niño canta. Y ella
      Da la cabeza hacia la calle
De Vera Cruz. Sus lágrimas

Se esconden, apenas, en la humedad
      De este mundo, una tierra
Que José Luís conoce, y por eso

Canta. Luís, tan listo, de once años.
      Luís, que ha cogido pesos
Desde la otra niñez ya perdida,

¿Sabrá que ha revolcado
      Un alma? El alma de esta joven,
Esta mujer que me ha estremecido

Con una mirada, con el susurro
      De una pregunta, queriendo respuestas
Sabias de su profesor. Otra bella,

Que no exige nada, pero que me hace exigir
      De mis palabras algo inútil.
Ella llora con el aullido callado

De reconocimiento—que el mundo
      Es pobre, y José Luís
Es del mundo. Yo conocía

Algo similar, hace muchos años,
　　　　Pero ya pasó. La vejez
Es una telaraña, hecha de puntos

De vista bien sazones, bien suaves.
　　　　Poco quiero: la curva de la piel,
Su muslo, la voz triste, el arco

De la espalda. Yo quiero
　　　　A su deseo, yo como de su anhelo,
El niño coge pesos. Yo quiero cantar.

Sin título

Busco la voz. Se ha escondido
Allí, bajo las piedras del cauce
De un agua fría, tremendamente fría.
Buena para la garganta, la sed
Esta, esta sed mía. Hecha
Por los aires de los desiertos míos
La sed me hace
Buscar, me manda la mano
Bajo el agua. Tiro las piedras
Con los dedos dolorosos, los huesos
Picados por las astillas
Del frío. Así voy yo, cazando
A la voz que es mi única. Tengo
Este derecho, el deber.

Oda a Selena

Es un día de puro Iowa.
El viento ataca la armazón.
Hay sol, pero no traspasa
la siembra de hielo
entre la nada blanca aquí y aquella allá.

El único calor
proviene del motor,
un aire metálico que reseca mi pelo,
que me hace grietas en la piel
de donde sale el espíritu del gringo,
silbando *no la escriba*.

No lucho tanto con el volumen.
No es tan difícil
dejarme caer en la telaraña
de su cabello. Azota el aire
cuando ella abre la boca
al micrófono, y canta disco
y luego mariachi, la borrachera
y tecno-cumbia.
No es duro olvidarme
de su muerte, aunque hay momentos
al lado de una finca sepultada de nieve,
con sus tractores en la bodega
y sus silos llenos de elote,
en que ella se pone suave la voz
y canta de sus sueños. Yo lloro, sabiendo
que esta cinta es mi vínculo
a su vida, una joven navajada
entre canciones. Ella, que se atreve
a ser ella, andando entre dos mundos
como si fueran uno, sus ambas palabras
volteándose en la misma frase, dos amantes

que se revuelcan tanto, hasta que sale
ella, entera, bella, lista a darme
paz y cachondez, que me revuelca
en este carro, riéndose
de mi humildad güera.

Que no me mueras, pues.

Sobreviviendo en Iowa

La razón por la cual
es el amor,
incestuoso como sea.
En este camino de elote
donde el maíz alimenta a la vaca,
es necesario. Aquí no hay raíz
propia. Oigo
a los cuentos ajenos
que se presentan
en un solo idioma.
No son míos, pues.

No hablo.
Sí leo, escribo, y si rezase,
pediría a diosito que me regale
una cantina de guanacos,
un par de momias
en la milpa, una esquina
de chapines que hagan amor
para tutear.

Para mientras, pues,
el libro y la pluma.
Construir puentes de papel
que me lleven
hasta el calor
del comal.

La piñata

Esta Pocahantas no se sangra
por ser una Barbie curtida y
hecha por Mickey Mouse.
Así me hablan los cipotes.
La quieren colgar del árbol
para que todos
gocen su turno.

Tronchan el aire del verano
con un palo entregado
por las millones de madres a las manos
de los inocentes.
Nunca entregan la historia, y así
despellejan la memoria.
El papel se cae
con los dulces atrapados.

Apenas ves los espíritus
de los güeros barbudos,
bailando bajo el indio
y su danza flotante.
La soga encoge el cuello.
El indio patea como conejo.
Los palos, machetes son.
Es fácil sacar la sangre dulce
y las tripas azucaradas de los primeros.
Que juguete, cecean, que cosa.

La risa de los niños
taja la visión.
Pocahantas baila sin quejarse.
Dale, dale, dale, no pierdas el ritmo,
Porque si lo pierdes, yo mato el indio.
Los pedazos morenos
se desparraman en mi yarda del olvido.

Oda a Derrida

Usted tiene arrebatados
los cráneos de estos poetas pobrecitos.
Ha hecho lobotomía
al pecho.
Discúlpeme, sí, yo sé:
no se puede existir tal cirugía,
aun si las palabras
son iguales de sentido, y por eso
no valen mierda.
Sí, tiene razón. La lobotomía
es para el cerebro. Y usted
no ha tocado nada de eso.

Pero ¡el corazón!
¿Dónde lo cuelga?
¿Con cuáles utensilios quirúrgicos
lo destripa?
Ey. No se me acerque,
o me voy de jolgorio
afuera, donde vuela la piñata
y la abuela comparte un chisme y
las tortillas se inflan en el comal.
Desconstruya *eso* (pendejo).

La cacería

Las flechas me amarran
a la tierra.
La bruma se levanta,
llevando mi última oración
de peras y mangos,
del beso y las yemas.
La congoja se suelta del cadáver.
Los cazadores me miran, como si yo
estuviese ensimismado, echando un vistazo
a los palos y las plumas.
El suspiro sale
por el tajo nuevo del pecho,
silbando por el hervor del corazón.

Sacan de las aljabas
botellitas de agua bendita
y me rocían.
Dicen otras palabras, arrebatando
la cosa que se llama alma, sellándole
de la tinta del imprimátur.
Uno pone su bota de charol
en mi ombligo
para arrancar la flecha.
Las navajas dejan una estela
de tripa y de carne.

Luego me dejan en paz.
Salen, y no me ven.

Mis ojos quedan abiertos.

Vienen la hojarasca
y las flores rosadas,
una y otra vez.

Se me olvida lo que me preocupaba,
aquel nido de zozobra que se llamaba
el día de sol, la noche de lluvia, el cipote riente,
mi mujer lista, las tortillas frescas.
¿Quién seguirá besando la tierra?
¿Cúya idea fue esta?

El viento baila con las plumas.
Ya se salió el hálito de arrobo.
Aquí todo es callado. Mis dedos,
Como palitos de tiza,
Desean dibujar en aquella pizarra azul.

El bisturí

Ya se apesta la llaga.
El olor cuelga en el aire
del culto
con el humo de las velas.
Apenas veo
los ademanes de los creyentes,
debido a las olas del tufo
que suben de mi herida.
Ya.

¿Quién me prestaría el bisturí?
Olvídate de eso.
La lesión gangrenosa
empieza bajo el corazón
y corre por el costado
hasta la ingle.
No tengo que tajar a nada. Ya se reventó
hace algunos días, mientras me persignaba.

Salen los primeros materiales
que se amontonaron desde la niñez:
Los abalorios negros metidos en la vejiga,
las hojas arrugadas en el intestino grueso
(la mancha de tinta
deja el evangelio
en la pared abdominal),
la hostia media digerida.
Ellos no son de la raíz.
Que lástima, pues. Que pena.

Allí está. Arrebata
Mi columna.

Tiene años de crecimiento.

Apretuja los huesos con la fe.
Parece cancerosa.
Quiero darle un tajo

A ver si aúlla.
Tiembla el bisturí en la mano.
En la carne muerta
no hay dolor.
Pero al arrancar el tubérculo mojado
de la vértebra, y cuando
el acero raspa la pared
llena de sangre latiente

y los pedazos de la carne buena
salen con la mala.

Oda al catarro

Hay algo del momento de yacer por horas y días
Sin moverte, y sentir el pulso de la fiebre
Que vibra y no vibra por la frente, dentro
Del abdomen, hasta la punta
Del pie izquierdo. Es como el gusto
De la marijuana de antes, sin el hambre
De ayer y con la tos de hoy. Así yo paso
Por el Museo de Las Artes de Latinoamérica
De Long Beach. Las estatuas de los maricones
Son bien chulas. Hombre en cuclillas.
Hombre erizado, hombre atado
A los cuatro puntos del globo, hay que duro es!
El escalofrío es una ráfaga de luto
Y de hallazgos. No encuentro nada
Ni nadie. Así la soledad sabe
Acariciarte. Sabe lamerte
Con la yema de una lengua
Manchada. No hay que hacer un romance
Del catarro. Todos sabemos
Que es pura fachada. La tos
Es tos. No hay hierba para fumar
Y el trago te hace más jodido.
El mareo es gratis. El sudor
Viene con la oferta. Por el deseo de morir
Te cobran extra. ¿Cómo vas a pedir
Por tanto? Las estatuas de los maricones
De Monterrey te prometen algo, te dicen
Que todo es posible bajo la respiración
Febril. Súbete aquí cabrón,
Encima de este caballero, o enfrente
De sus nalgas. Respira algo nuevo.
La fiebre te da derecho, y nosotros

Te empinamos y así todos salimos
Pijudos y nuevecitos. Tú bien agachado,
Y yo, sí, yo, aquí, el más grande
Y acuclillado, ya como me has adorado.

End It

The dreams are all folly.
          They dance about in the offal
of childhood, a bathroom for a boy
          age eight. There he will drown.
The mother and the father, both are near,
          dragging from cigarettes in the kitchen
behind him. And the older brother passes by
          in a flash. It always happens this way,
when you choose not to drink. When the evening draught
          is not there, your nights are more real
than day. It is the real that vexes,
          the question of which to choose: this,
which created the blue toilet, the river of shit
          in the dream, or the dream itself,
which means reflections are real. The mirror image
          means more.

                    Reading Márquez once again,
Cien años. How José Arcadio Buendía
          runs from the man he killed, builds
Macondo, spreads his seed, and still
          Prudencio returns, cleaning out
the bleeding cut in his neck, weeping over
          José's thrown spear. There is no escape
from the past. But that's a teaching,
          as if Gabo ever meant to teach.
Gabo's world is more real than my own.
          My abuela could have told me that,
the day she dug up the bones of her husband
          and tossed them on the bones of her dead,
hated brother-in-law, and explained in a now-famous curse,
          "He fucked my husband all his life.
Now it's my man's turn." Piling bones on bones,
          for my people, both here and in

El Salvador, takes care of everything.
          Watching every single night
a toilet overflow—what good is that?
          What good is the reminder that you
will not escape? And would you want that?
          Were all that to disappear, you know
what would happen: a puff of smoke,
          hardly that. Oh, just another apology,
another line scratched out, another nail to hit.
          More symbols. Pile them on,
as if they were real.

About the Author

Marcos McPeek Villatoro is the author of several books of fiction, poetry, and nonfiction. The *Los Angeles Times Book Review* listed his nationally acclaimed *Home Killings: A Romilia Chacón Mystery* as one of their "Best Books of 2001." It also won the Silver Medal from *Foreword* magazine and first prize in the Latino Literary Hall of Fame.

His novel *The Holy Spirit of My Uncle's Cojones* was an Independent Publishers Book Award Finalist and was nominated for the Pushcart Prize. His other books include *They Say That I Am Two: Poems, A Fire in the Earth*, and the memoir *Walking to La Milpa: Living in Guatemala with Armies, Demons, Abrazos, and Death. Minos: A Romilia Chacón Mystery*, was released in the fall of 2003.

After he graduated from the Iowa Writers' Workshop in 1998, Villatoro and his family moved to Los Angeles, where he holds the Fletcher Jones Endowed Chair in Writing at Mount St. Mary's College.

Villatoro hosts a program on Pacifica Radio in Los Angeles called *Shelf-Life*, where he interviews other novelists and poets from across the country. He also does commentary for National Public Radio. He lives with his wife and four children in the San Fernando Valley.